IN PRAISE OF KRISHNA

IN PRAISE OF KRISHNA
Songs from the Bengali

Translated by
Edward C. Dimock, Jr., and Denise Levertov

With an Introduction and Notes by
Edward C. Dimock, Jr.

Illustrations by Anju Chaudhuri

THE UNIVERSITY OF CHICAGO PRESS
CHICAGO AND LONDON

This edition published by arrangement with Doubleday & Company, Inc., and the Asia Society, Inc.

The following poems first appeared in *Poetry*, copyright © 1965 by Modern Poetry Association: O Madhava, how shall I tell you of my terror?; Beloved, what more shall I say to you; My mind is not on housework; I who body and soul; As water to sea-creatures; Let the earth of my body be mixed with the earth. Others appeared in *The East-West Review* 1966, copyright © 1966 by The East-West Review.

The University of Chicago Press, Chicago 60637
The University of Chicago Press, Ltd., London

© 1967 by the Asia Society, Inc.
All rights reserved. Published 1967
Paperback edition 1981
Printed in the United States of America
04 03 02 01 00 99   6 7 8 9

ISBN: 0-226-15231-6

Library of Congress Cataloging in Publication Data
Main entry under title:

In praise of Krishna.

   Reprint. Originally published: 1st ed. Garden City, N.Y.: Doubleday, 1967. (UNESCO collection of
representative works: Indian series)
   Bibliography: p.
   1. Bengali poetry—Translations into English.
2. English poetry—Translations from Bengali.
3. Krishna (Hindu deity)—Poetry. I. Dimock, Edward C. II. Levertov, Denise, 1923– . III. Series: Unesco collection of representative works: Indian series.
PK1771.E315   1981   891'.441'0080382   81-3419

∞ The paper used in this publication meets the minimum requirements of the American National Standard for Information Sciences—Permanence of Paper for Printed Library Materials, ANSI Z39.48–1984.

ACKNOWLEDGMENTS

We want to express our thanks to the Asian Literature Program of the Asia Society for its support, and particularly to Mrs. Bonnie R. Crown, the Director of the Program, first for her suggestion that such a book as this one should be prepared, and secondly for her advice and constant encouragement in its preparation.

Our thanks also go to Miss Roushan Jahan, a graduate student at the University of Chicago who is working on various aspects of Vaishnava poetry, for the use of certain selections and preliminary translations which she made for another purpose; and to various friends, scholars, and poets in Calcutta, especially Dr. Naresh Guha of Jadavpur University and Mr. Abu Sayeed Ayyub, editor of *Quest*, with whom some of the translations were discussed and dissected. If there are any errors of translation or interpretation, the knowledge and sensibility of these and other friends is not at fault.

Our acknowledgment of the various texts which we have used for translation is given in the section called "On Translation and Transliteration."

INTRODUCTION

Above the highest heaven is the dwelling place of Krishna. It is a place of infinite idyllic peace, where the dark and gentle river Yamunā flows beside a flowered meadow, where cattle graze; on the river's bank sweet-scented trees blossom and bend their branches to the earth, where peacocks dance and nightingales call softly. Here Krishna, ever-young, sits beneath the trees, the sound of his flute echoing the nightingales' call. Sometimes he laughs and jokes and wrestles with his friends, sometimes he teases the cowherd-girls of the village, the Gopīs, as they come to the river for water. And sometimes, in the dusk of days an eon long, his flute's call summons the Gopīs to his side. They leave their homes and families and husbands and honor—as it is called by men—and go to him. Their love for him is deeper than their fear of dishonor. He is the fulfillment of all desire. The loveliest and most beloved of the Gopīs is one called Rādhā.

It is told in ancient Hindu texts that once, long, long ago, this Krishna came to earth, and with him came all the things and people of his heaven—the river, the cows, the peacocks and nightingales, and the Gopīs who love him. And as this story is sometimes interpreted, there took place in Vrindāvana (on modern maps of India, southeast of Delhi), in a kind of microtime, all that is happening eternally in the source, the heavenly Vrindāvana. And, it is said, ==all this is what takes place in the human heart: the Gopīs' love for Krishna is the love of man for God.==

It is man's nature to long for that which is most beautiful: the gentlest of sounds, the most radiant color, the sweetest scent, his whole body for that which is most tender and full of grace. The sound of Krishna's flute is gentlest. His body, glowing like a blue jewel, is most radiant. His scent is sweetest. And the grace of his posture and the tenderness of his love are the most soothing, and most exciting, to the heart which yearns. Rādhā longs for utter union with her divine and emerald-colored (*shyāma*, dark-colored) lover:

> Let the earth of my body be mixed with the earth
> my beloved walks on.
> Let the fire of my body be the brightness
> in the mirror that reflects his face.
> Let the water of my body join the waters
> of the lotus pool he bathes in.
> Let the breath of my body be air
> lapping his tired limbs.
> Let me be sky, and moving through me
> that cloud-dark Shyāma, my beloved.

The use of such multileveled imagery should not be surprising. Those who have an acquaintance with the poetry of the Sufis of Islam will find it familiar. The great Persian Sufi poet Ḥāfiẓ of Shīrāz writes:

> Though I be old, clasp me one night to thy breast,
> and I, when the dawn shall come to awaken me,

with the flush of youth on my cheek from thy bosom will rise.[1]

Or, closer to home, there is the love poetry of the *Song of Songs,* sometimes interpreted rightly or wrongly as an allegory of love between human and divine. There are the enigmatic songs of the troubadours. There are the considerations of St. Bernard, among many others, to whom the soul of man is the Bride

> to be introduced by the King into His chamber, to be united with Him, to enjoy Him . . .[2]

And still closer, at least in time, there are the musings of Gerard Manley Hopkins and his friend Coventry Patmore, in the age of Victoria, especially in Patmore's "Ode to the Body" and in his lost "Sponsa Dei."[3] In all of these, physical and metaphysical imagery interweave and mingle, until one is no longer quite sure whether to read the poem as poetry or as doctrine. Or whether to try to avoid the question altogether. Von Grunebaum, writing of the earthy imagery employed by the Sufi poets, discerns that third possibility:

> The break between reality and symbol, sound and meaning, is overcome by projecting the ex-

[1] Translated by G. L. Bell, *Poems from the Divan of Hafiz* (London, 1897), pp. 118–19; quoted in Gustave E. von Grunebaum, *Medieval Islam* (University of Chicago Phoenix Books, 1961), p. 293.
[2] *Sermones de diversis VIII: 9;* quoted Maurice Valency, *In Praise of Love* (New York: Macmillan, 1961), p. 22.
[3] See Herbert Read, *Collected Essays in Literary Criticism* (London: Faber and Faber, 2nd edition 1950), p. 327.

perience of the soul onto both the planes on which, to the Persian poet, human life is lived. When Hafiz (d. 1390) sings of wine and love, or the intoxication with the One that inspires his verse—the two motives are inextricably joined. Earthly and heavenly longing are but aspects of the same aspiration. The ambiguity of the imagery exists only on the surface. The poet may be pleased to puzzle and mislead the ignorant; but ultimately the two-sidedness of his words reflects the two-sidedness of man's situation in the universe. As long as he lives, he expresses himself in terms of his lower nature; but, stripped of his bodily chains, he belongs with the Eternal whence he issued and whither he is to return.[4]

The burning of human love and longing comes, in poetry at least, from a spark of the divine; man's "yearning for a twin of flesh," as one of the Vaishnava poets says, is a reflection of some primordial, long-forgotten lust, and pain of separation.

In the period from the fourteenth through the seventeenth centuries a great *bhakti* (enthusiastic and devotional) movement swept across northern and eastern India; the Vaishnava lyrics of Bengal represent one of the ways in which this enthusiasm found expression. But although the creative peak of the Bengali Vaishnava lyric poetry was in the sixteenth and seventeenth centuries, this poetry is as much a part of living tradition as some Christian hymnody of the same period. The comparison is in fact not as farfetched as it might sound, for the Vaishnava lyrics are in intent devotional, they are

[4] von Grunebaum, loc. cit.

x

meant to be sung, and they are not limited to the Vaishnava sect, but are the valued property of all Bengalis. They are sung by Vaishnavas in a form of worship called *kīrtan,* which means, simply, "praise." One must imagine a scene like this:

It is evening, in a village in Bengal. The sodden heat of the day has not yet passed, and clothes still stick to backs, though only the faintest glow lingers in the western sky, only enough to make palm trees show in silhouette. On the veranda floor of a temple of Krishna men are seated, their faces lit by the glare of a gas pressure-lantern placed near the center of the circle. Women are off to one side, and can be seen darkly against the light of oil lamps burning by the image of Krishna and the long-eyed Rādhā. He, Krishna, is deep blue-green in color, dressed in yellow robes with a garland of flowers round his neck, his flute in his right hand, his right leg bent and crossed in front of his left; his left arm is around Rādhā, who is beautiful, the color of melted gold. A long cylindrical drum rests across the knees of one of the men, its two heads differing in size; as the man's right hand marks quick, intricate rhythms, his left hand punctuates them more slowly, more deeply, though with equal delicacy. Another man plays a pair of small cymbals, harsh and hypnotizing.

The leader of the *kīrtan* party, nearest the center of the circle, has begun to sing the type of lyric called *Gaurachandrikā*—a hymn to the great fifteenth-century Vaishnava saint Chaitanya (Gaura, "the Golden One"), whom some reverence as an incarnation of Krishna, some as Krishna himself, and some as Rādhā and Krishna in one body, in the most intimate possible embrace; it has been said that a

Gaurachandrikā must be sung first, to set the proper mood, and to prevent any misinterpretation of the sometimes sensual imagery of the Rādhā-Krishna songs which are to follow.

The leader sings the first couplet of the *Gaurachandrikā*, and the rest repeat it in chorus. The melody is, to unaccustomed ears, shrill and subtle: it seems as if a musical phrase is never repeated. But after long listening, it is clear that the melodies and rhythms of the couplets, and of each song, are closely defined. One of the restrictions upon the composer of these lyrics, as upon the composer of a sonnet, is that he must work within carefully delineated metrical and musical boundaries, as well as boundaries of image; within such limits, poetic brilliance is easily discerned.

The introductory *Gaurachandrikās* have been sung. People have been coming and going—mostly, it would seem, coming, moving in and out of the shadow, against the oil lamps, and now the group has grown quite large. They begin to sing: first of the boy Krishna, playing in the fields, dancing in the courtyard of his foster-mother's house while the women and girls of the town crowd around, entranced by his grace and beauty; then they sing of the loveliness of Rādhā, of the goldenness of her body, delicate and quick as a lightning flash; then of Krishna's desire for her, and the first shy, solemn meeting of the lovers; they sing of Rādhā's jealousy at the thought of Krishna's lovemaking with other Gopīs, and her feigned anger, and of the messengers who carry back and forth between the two tales of Krishna's repentance and Rādhā's regret and renewed longing. They sing songs of the beauty of the love of Rādhā and Krishna, and of their dark and golden bodies coming together. Perhaps a man, or several men, knowing then the love of the Gopīs for Krishna, knowing the unselfish pleasure of Rādhā's friends at the union of the lovers, perhaps knowing even the experience of Rādhā's love itself, stand up to dance. It is deep in the night. The faces of the singers and musicians are lined with concentration and streaked with sweat. They are Gopīs, and the eternal love of Rādhā and Krishna is as immediate as the songs they sing of it.

Finally, they sing of Krishna's departure from the fields of Vrindāvana to go to the city of Mathurā; in songs of separation, which are among the finest and most moving of all, they speak their longing. The pique, the passion, the anger and satisfaction, the union and the separation, and above all the willingness to give up everything for the sake of the Beloved, trace the course of true love, between man and woman, and between man and God.

Those who are familiar with Krishna's name through such texts as the *Bhagavād Gītā* may be a little surprised to find him, in the greater part of the thought and literature of the Vaishnavas of Bengal, as the lover rather than the warrior hero. Those who have heard of the so-called "Hindu trinity" (Brahmā "the creator," Shiva "the destroyer," and Vishnu "the preserver") may be equally surprised to find that in the Bengali texts Krishna is himself the great god, not a mere incarnation of Vishnu the third member of this triad, as he is sometimes considered elsewhere in Indian religion. Krishna, like most of India's deities, has many aspects, an obscure genealogy, and certain unexpected characteristics (for instance, he is dark, despite the fact that fairness is generally considered a mark of beauty in India).

Some scholars feel that Krishna was originally the tribal hero of a central Indian pastoral people, who in the course of time became associated with deities who had normal divine functions, such as the slaying of demons and the preservation of the moral order. As myths and legends of other gods and heroes attached themselves to Krishna, his character acquired many of their attributes.

Whatever the validity of this theory, one does find many kinds of Krishna in the texts. In the *Mahābhārata* Krishna is a prince, friend, and adviser to the Pandavas, one of the factions of the great war described in that epic. In that section of the *Mahābhārata* called the *Bhagavād Gītā*, we find Krishna not only counseling Arjuna while he searches his soul for a proper course of action in a battle against friends and relatives, but revealing himself as God. And in the *Bhāgavata Purāna* itself, Krishna is the youthful, desirable lover of the Gopīs, and the slayer of the demon king Kamśa, who had, in a striking parallel to a Christian story, ordered a slaughter of innocents. In the same text we find Krishna, the child god and the great king, the husband of Rukmini.

But of all these aspects, the most significant for the Vaishnavas of Bengal was Krishna the lover and the beloved, whose foremost characteristic is the giving and receiving of joy, who is approachable only by *bhakti*, by devotion and selfless dedication.

One of the characteristics of the *bhakti* movement was the use of regional languages rather than Sanskrit for most of the poetic, biographical, and even theological literature which it inspired. Thus, the great *bhakta* poet Tukarām wrote in Marathi, a language spoken today in western India in the area around Bombay, the equally great Kabir in Hindi, the present language of a great part of northern India, and most of the poets represented in this book in Bengali, a vigorous eastern descendant of Sanskrit which began to assert its independence around the tenth century A.D. (The language of most of those non-Bengali poems here represented is Brajabuli, an artificial language compounded of Bengali and a type of eastern Hindi; this knew no life outside the corpus of the songs of the Vaishnavas. A few of the Vaishnava lyrics are in Sanskrit itself.) This is a technical but significant fact, for during this period, Sanskrit had for all intents and purposes become the property of the "churchmen," the religious specialists of the dominant and restrictive Brahmanical priestly tradition. The poets of the *bhakti* movement spoke not to the followers of the rigid and determinist Brahmanical tradition, but to people who believed that the path to salvation lay in devotion to God, people whose satisfactions under the Brahmanical system were slight. To reach this group, often untutored in the "language of culture," Sanskrit, these poets used for the most part the languages of everyday. And because these languages had vitality, the songs of the *bhakti* poets have a directness not common in late classical Sanskrit.

On the other hand, the debt of the Bengali Vaishnava lyrics to their prolific Sanskrit progenitor is clear in other ways. Many of them use metrical patterns found in Sanskrit, and rhyme schemes used by such late classical Sanskrit writers as Jayadeva in his *Gītagovinda*[5] (earlier Sanskrit did not employ regularly recurrent rhyme). The imagery used by the Vaishnavas is often the stylized imagery of Sanskrit court poetry: their lyrics abound in *chakora* birds—fictitious birds which live on moonbeams, in lotuses and peacocks and all the other paraphernalia of the idyllic scenes of the Rādhā-Krishna story. And the various epithets of Rādhā and Krishna and the others who populate the lyrics have reference, of course, to earlier Sanskrit stories and texts. A god in India is called by many names, depending upon the capacity in which he is being worshiped at a particular time, the feeling of the worshiper toward him, the place in which, in a particular aspect, he is thought to dwell, his color and shape, a particular feat of demon-killing which he may have accomplished, and a great many other variables. "The bodiless one" is thus Kāma, the god of love, who had been burned up by the wrath of Shiva when he attempted to seduce that great god from meditation. Kāma is also, for more obvious reasons, "the mind-born one." Krishna may be "he-who-holds-the-mountain," a reference to Krishna's holding the mountain Govardhana on his little finger over the heads of the villagers to protect them from the angry Indra's storm or Mādhava, the great god, slayer of demons. Krishna may also be Shyāma, "the dark-colored one," whose complexion is dark as a peacock's neck, or the waves of the Yamunā river, or the storm cloud which brings relief and joy to the people of

[5] A work several times translated into English, most recently and most elegantly by Barbara Stoler Miller, *Love Song of the Dark Lord* (New York: Columbia University Press, 1977). Jayadeva was a poet at the court of Lakshmana Sena of Bengal about A.D. 1200. The *Gītagovinda* is a series of highly erotic lyrics on the Rādhā-Krishna theme.

the scorched plains. He may also be called Kān or Kānu. Rādhā may be "the golden one," the setting for the emerald of Krishna's body, or Rai, an intimate and affectionate name. Her face is like the full moon, a traditional metaphor for beauty; it gladdens the eyes of all observers as the moon gladdens *chakora* birds starved for its light.

As the imagery of these poems can be—indeed, must be—read on at least two levels at once, so must any translation from a language embodying a culture basically unfamiliar to speakers of English be read on several levels. The first level is of course that of whatever pleasure may be aroused and stimulated by the English as poetry. The second level is more abstruse, for it has to do with the notion that translation is basically impossible, becoming increasingly so with the distance of the translated language from English. A Bengali, because of his Bengaliness, has reactions and associations with words and rhythms and images which a speaker of English can never have. One criterion of the selection of these poems has been, then, intelligibility to the Westerner. But intelligibility will not be complete even then, for Indian poets of this period wrote with the *sahṛdaya* in mind, "the man of sensibility," meaning sensibility to the particular chain of associations which the poet could arouse in the minds of people from his own tradition. For example, here is a lyric by "Vidyāpati," which is a favorite of non-Vaishnava Bengalis as well as those who belong to the Vaishnava sect:

> O my friend, my sorrow is unending.
> It is the rainy season, my house is empty,
> the sky is filled with seething clouds,
> the earth sodden with rain,

and my love far away.
Cruel Kāma pierces me with his arrows:
the lightning flashes, the peacocks dance,
frogs and waterbirds, drunk with delight,
call incessantly—and my heart is heavy.
Darkness on earth,
the sky intermittently lit with a sullen glare . . .

*Vidyāpati says,
how will you pass this night without your lord?*

The rainy season is the time for lovers, the time when the earth is lush and green again, when the wind is filled with the scent of sandalwood. It is poignant, when lovers are apart. The arrows of Kāma are flowers, sharpened by longing. "Kāma," when not a proper name, means "sexual desire." And, finally, the poet's signature line (a practice common to the poets of this period) climactically offers a whole second interpretation to the poem: is the lady, probably Rādhā, longing for her absent lover, or does she call for a divine lord to help her pass the dark night of the soul, to help her deny the lusts of the flesh?

Most of the lyrics of the Bengal Vaishnavas are in the mood called *mādhurya-bhāva,* in which the poet is considering Krishna in his aspect of divine lover; he writes as if he himself were Rādhā or one of the Gopīs. Reflecting the fondness for classification and typing for which Indian thought is well known, the Vaishnavas say that the *mādhurya-bhāva* songs are divided into two broad categories: *vipralambha,* the lovers in separation, and *sambhoga,* the lovers' enjoyment in union. The point is, however, that these two categories are not entirely separable, for separation is latent in union, and union latent in separation, as death is latent in life. *Vipralambha* is in its turn divided into four main subsections:

a. *pūrva-rāga*, in which condition desire is aroused in each of the lovers by sight and by listening to descriptions of the other.

b. *māna*, a condition in which the girl feels that an offense against her honor has been committed, that her pride has been injured, especially because her lover has been paying attention to other women.

c. *premavaicittya*, a condition in which simultaneous satisfaction and pain of longing are present: even though the lovers may be together, there is the realization that separation is not far off.

d. *pravāsa*, the pain of separation aroused in the girl because of her lover's departure to another country.

These categories are further subdivided according to their numerous possible variations.

In the Vaishnava anthologies and in *kīrtan*, the lyrics are arranged to reflect a human love affair against a metaphysical screen. So they are, with one or two minor liberties and the omission of some categories, in this book.

The lyrics of the Vaishnava sect have certain formal peculiarities. First, it was conventional among the Vaishnava poets to use what is known as a *bhanitā*, or signature line, which usually occurs at the end of a poem. In the *bhanitā*, the poet identifies himself by name, and, if he considers himself a participant in the poem, the poet addresses Rādhā or Krishna, or muses to himself. Often the *bhanitā* will bring the reader up short, offer him a completely new interpretation of the poem, and cause him to read it again. Sometimes the *bhanitā* is no more than a simple declaration: "So says Vidyapati," or whoever the poet may be. We have used our discretion in including the *bhanitā* depending on its relevance to the poem. Some we have left out completely. Others, which seem necessary to the poem, we have retained, but with the liberty of putting them in italics. Though we have not always included the *bhanitās,* it should not be forgotten that this motif is, in Bengali, a consistent convention.

SELECTED ENGLISH BIBLIOGRAPHY

Archer, W. G., *The Loves of Krishna in Indian Painting and Poetry* (New York: Grove Press, 1958), 2nd printing.

Bhattacharya, Deben (trans.), *Love Songs of Vidyapati,* with an introduction by William G. Archer (London: George Allen and Unwin, 1961).

Dasgupta, Shashibhusan, *Obscure Religious Cults* (Calcutta: K. L. Mukhopadhyaya, 1962), 2nd edition.

De, S. K., *Vaishnava Faith and Movement in Bengal* (Calcutta: K. L. Mukhopadhyaya, 1961), 2nd edition.

Dimock, Edward C., Jr., *The Place of the Hidden Moon: Erotic Mysticism in the Vaishnava Sahajiyā Cult of Bengal* (Chicago: University of Chicago Press, 1966).

Kennedy, Melville, *The Chaitanya Movement* (Calcutta: The Association Press, 1925).

Sen, Dinesh Chandra, *History of the Bengali Language and Literature* (Calcutta: Calcutta University Press, 1954), 2nd edition.

Sen, Sukumar, *A History of Brajabuli Literature* (Calcutta: Calcutta University Press, 1935).

Singer, Milton B. (ed.), *Krishna: Myths, Rites, and Attitudes* (Honolulu: East-West Center Press, 1966).

Thompson, Edward J. and A. M. Spencer, *Bengali Religious Lyrics: Vaishnava* (Calcutta: The Association Press, 1925).

Wilson, Frances (ed. and trans.), *The Love of Krishna* (Philadelphia: University of Pennsylvania Press, 1975).

Gaurachandrikā

*Hymns to Gaurachandra,
the Golden Moon, the Lord Chaitanya*

*After long sorrow, I am graciously
brought by fate to my Golden One,
my Gaura,
my treasury of virtue.
After long sorrow I am brought to joy,
my eyes learn what their vision is for,
looking into his face, bright moon.
A long time they were fasting, my eyes,
those thirsty* chakora *birds whose sole food
is moonbeams:
now they have found
the round moon itself!*

Vāsudeva Ghosh sings to his Gaura, his Golden One,
like a man blind from birth who has found his sight.

It was in bitter maytime my lord
renounced the world, and shaved his head,
and took to the roads with only a
staff and a begging bowl.
My heart sickens, tears
sting my eyes. The hope of my life
went with him.
How long will my days drag on
without him, my Gaura?
The springtime, when the world brims over
with joy, comes round again,
bitter to me.
My old love for my lord
aches in my heart, all I remember
makes life a noose
tightening about my throat.

Rāmānanda says, He was the lord of my life.
When shall I see him, with Gadādhara, again?

Pūrva-rāga

The awakening of love between
Krishna and Rādhā

The girl and the woman
bound in one being:
the girl puts up her hair,
the woman lets it
fall to cover her breasts;
the girl reveals her arms,
her long legs, innocently bold;
the woman wraps her shawl modestly about her,
her open glance a little veiled.
Restless feet, a blush on the young breasts,
hint at her heart's disquiet:
behind her closed eyes
Kāma awakes, born in imagination, the god.

*Vidyāpati says, O Krishna, bridegroom,
be patient, she will be brought to you.*

He speaks:

Her slender body like a flash of lightning,
her feet, color of dawn, stepping swiftly
among the other lotus petals . . .
Friend, tell me who she is! She plays
among her friends,
plays with my heart.
When she raises her eyebrows I see
the arching waves of the River Kālindī.
Her careless look lights on a leaf
and the whole forest flames into blue flowers.
When she smiles
a delicate sweetness fills me, fragrance
of lily and jasmine.

O Kān, you are bewitched:
Do you not know your Rāi?

Prathama milan

The first meeting of Rādhā and Krishna

Fingering the border of her friend's sari, nervous and
                afraid,
sitting tensely on the edge of Krishna's couch,

as her friend left she too looked to go
but in desire Krishna blocked her way.

He was infatuated, she bewildered;
he was clever, and she naive.

He put out his hand to touch her; she quickly pushed
                it away.
He looked into her face, her eyes filled with tears.

He held her forcefully, she trembled violently
and hid her face from his kisses behind the edge of
                her sari.

Then she lay down, frightened, beautiful as a doll;
he hovered like a bee round a lotus in a painting.

Govinda-dāsa says, Because of this,
drowned in the well of her beauty,
Krishna's lust was changed.

Anurāga

In which Rādhā describes the depth of her love

As the mirror to my hand,
the flowers to my hair,
kohl to my eyes,
tāmbul to my mouth,
musk to my breast,
necklace to my throat,
ecstasy to my flesh,
heart to my home—

as wing to bird,
water to fish,
life to the living—
so you to me.
But tell me,
Mādhava, beloved,
who are you?
Who are you really?

Vidyāpati says, they are one another.

Love, I take on splendor in your splendor,
grace and gentleness are mine because of your beauty.

I remember
how I embraced your feet, holding them
tight to my breast.

Others have many loves, I have
only you,
dearer to me than life.
You are the kohl on my eyes, the ornaments
on my body,
you, dark moon.

*Jñāna-dāsa says, Your love
binds heart to heart.*

As water to sea creatures,
    moon nectar to *chakora* birds,
    companionable dark to the stars—
my love is to Krishna.

My body hungers for his
    as mirror image hungers
    for twin of flesh.

His life cuts into my life
    as the stain of the moon's rabbit
    engraves the moon.

As if a day when no sun came up
    and no color came to the earth—
that's how it is in my heart when he goes away.

*Vidyāpati says, Cherish such love
and keep it young, fortunate girl.*

My friend, I cannot answer when you ask me to
                    explain
what has befallen me.
Love is transformed, renewed,
each moment.
He has dwelt in my eyes all the days of my life,
yet I am not sated with seeing.
My ears have heard his sweet voice in eternity,
and yet it is always new to them.
How many honeyed nights have I passed with him
in love's bliss, yet my body
wonders at his.
Through all the ages
he has been clasped to my breast,
yet my desire
never abates.
I have seen subtle people sunk in passion
but none came so close to the heart of the fire.

*Who shall be found to cool your heart,
says Vidyāpati.*

Milan

Rādhā goes to meet Krishna
in the trysting place

O Mādhava, how shall I tell you of my terror?
I could not describe my coming here
if I had a million tongues.
When I left my room and saw the darkness
I trembled:
I could not see the path,
there were snakes that writhed round my ankles!

I was alone, a woman; the night was so dark,
the forest so dense and gloomy,
and I had so far to go.
The rain was pouring down—
which path should I take?
My feet were muddy
and burning where thorns had scratched them.
But I had the hope of seeing you, none of it mattered,
and now my terror seems far away . . .
When the sound of your flute reaches my ears
it compels me to leave my home, my friends,
it draws me into the dark toward you.

*I no longer count the pain of coming here,
says Govinda-dāsa.*

This dark cloudy night
he'll not come to me . . .
But yes, he is here!
He stands dripping with rain
in the courtyard. O my heart!

What virtue accrued in
another life has brought me
such bliss? I who
fear my elders and dare not go out to him?
I who torment him? I see

his sorrow and deep love
and I am tormented.
I would set fire to my house
for him, I would bear
the scorn of the world.

He thinks his sorrow is joy,
when I weep he weeps.

When it comes to know such depth of love
the heart of the world will rejoice,
says Chandidāsa.

When they had made love
she lay in his arms in the *kunja* grove.
Suddenly she called his name
and wept—as if she burned in the fire of
separation.
                  The gold was in her *anchal*
                  but she looked afar for it!
—Where has he gone? Where has my love gone?
O why has he left me alone?
And she writhed on the ground in despair,
only her pain kept her from fainting.
Krishna was astonished
and could not speak.

Taking her beloved friend by the hand,
Govinda-dāsa led her softly away.

Lord of my heart, what have I dreamed . . .
how shall I go home, now that daylight has come?
My musk and sandalwood perfumes are faded,
the kohl smudged from my eyes, the vermilion line
drawn in the part of my hair, paled.
O put the ornament
of your own body upon me,
take me with you, down-glancing one.
Dress me in your own yellow robes,
smooth my disheveled hair,
wind round my throat your garland of forest flowers.
Thus, beloved, someone in Gokula entreats.

Basu Rāmānanda says, Such is your love
that deer and tiger are together in your dwelling
place.

Ākṣepānurāga

Rādhā is regretful that she has given herself to Krishna, and resentful of his power over her. She speaks:

With the last of my garments
shame dropped from me, fluttered
to earth and lay discarded at my feet.
My lover's body became
the only covering I needed.
With bent head he gazed at the lamp
like a bee who desires the honey of a closed lotus.
The Mind-stealing One, like the *chātaka* bird,
is wanton, he misses no chance
to gratify his thirst: I was to him
a pool of raindrops.
                Now shame returns
as I remember. My heart trembles,
recalling his treachery.

So Vidyāpati says.

To her friend:

O, why did I go to the Yamunā river? There
the moon apple of Nanda's eye lay waiting
under the *kadamba* tree.
The honey of his look, the radiance
of his body—these
were the bait and the snare he laid:
and my eyes lit there like birds
and at once were trapped,
and my heart leapt like a doe into his nets
leaving the cage of my breast empty,
and goaded by his glance,
my pride, that wild elephant,
which I had kept
chained night and day in my mind, broke loose
and escaped me.
            At the first note of his flute
down came the lion gate of reverence for elders,
down came the door of *dharma*,
my guarded treasure of modesty was lost,
I was thrust to the ground as if by a thunderbolt.
Ah, yes, his dark body
poised in the *tribhanga* pose
shot the arrow that pierced me;
no more honor, my family
lost to me,
my home at Vraja
lost to me.
Only my life is left—and my life too
is only a breath that is leaving me.

So says Jagadānanda-dāsa.

To her friend:

How can I describe his relentless flute,
which pulls virtuous women from their homes
and drags them by their hair to Shyām
as thirst and hunger pull the doe to the snare?
Chaste ladies forget their lords,
wise men forget their wisdom,
and clinging vines shake loose from their trees,
hearing that music.
Then how shall a simple dairymaid withstand its call?

Chandidāsa says, Kālā the puppetmaster leads the dance.

To her friend:

My mind is not on housework.
Now I weep, now I laugh at the world's
censure.
      He draws me—to become
an outcast, a hermit woman in the woods!
He has bereft me of parents, brothers, sisters,
my good name. His flute
took my heart—
his flute, a thin bamboo trap enclosing me—
a cheap bamboo flute was Rādhā's ruin.
That hollow, simple stick—
fed nectar by his lips, but issuing
poison . . .

If you should find
a clump of jointed reeds,
pull off their branches!
Tear them up by the roots!
Throw them
            into the sea.

Dvija Chandidāsa says, Why the bamboo?
Not it but Krishna enthralls you: him you cannot
                 uproot.

To herself:

I brought honey and drank it mixed with milk—
but where was its sweetness? I tasted gall.
I am steeped in bitterness, as the seed
of a bitter fruit in its juice.
My heart smolders.
A fire without is plain to be seen
but this fire flames within,
it sears my breast.
Desire burns the body—how can it be relieved?

By the touch of Kānu, says Chandidāsa.

To Krishna:

Love, what can I say to you?
I was too young to love,
but you did not let me stay at home.
I shall drown myself in the sea
with this last wish:
that I be born again as Nanda's son
and you as Rādhā.
Then, after loving you, I shall abandon you.
I shall stand beneath the *kadamba* tree;
I shall stand in the *tribhanga* pose and play my flute
as you go to draw water.
And when you hear the flute you will be enchanted,
simple girl.

*Chandidāsa says, Then you will know
how love can burn.*

To Krishna:

A wicked woman—fouler than the foulest poison.
So his mother's cruelty, like fire
burning in me.
My tyrant husband: the whetted
edge of a razor. And all around me,
reproachful dutiful women.
My love, what shall I tell you?
Whatever their calumnies, you
are my life itself.
           My body
bears your brand—they know it.
For shame I cannot raise my head
              before chaste women,
I cannot bear the cruelty, the knife-thrust
of seeing my fellow women make mocking signs to
              me.
I have weighed it all.
              Yet I have chosen
to endure abuse for your sake.

So Balarāma-dāsa says.

Āptadūtī

Krishna sends a messenger, an old woman, to Rādhā, to tell of his misery, to plead with her to come to him again

The messenger speaks:

I place beauty spots on my sagging cheeks,
smudge kohl around my dulling eyes,
put flowers in my burned-white hair.
Yes, my vanity is absurd,
the years have slipped by,
I remember, and grieve for them;
my breasts hang limp,
my hips are bony.
Yet on this withered body
the God of Love plunges and rolls.

She speaks to Rādhā:

Shining one, golden as the *champa* flower,
the god of fate has given your radiance to you
in sacred offering.
Fortunate one, blessed and golden one,
his dark body shall wed with yours.
Waste nothing of the light of youth,
go quickly to him.

And Lochana, entreating, says,
if you go you save the life of Shyām.

Māna
(*Kalahāntaritā*)

Rādhā, separated from her lover and unhappy but still angry, replies

She addresses the messenger:

From the time our eyes first met
our longing grew.
He was not only the desirer, I not only the desired:
passion ground our hearts together in its mortar.
Friend, do not forget to recall to Krishna
how it was with us then.
Then we required no messenger, sought
only each other's lips for our love.
It was the god of love himself who united us,
he of the five arrows . . .
But now my lordly lover has learned new manners,
now he sends *you,* herald of his indifference!

So, with anger like a king's, increasing,
sings the poet Rāmānanda Rāy.

The messenger replies:

When you listened to the sound
of Krishna's flute,
I stopped your ears.
When you gazed at the beauty
of his body,
I covered your eyes.
You were angry.
O lovely one, I told you then
that if you let love grow in you
your life would pass in tears.
You offered him your body,
you wanted his touch—
you did not ask if he would be kind.
And now each day your beauty
fades a little more;
how much longer can you live?
You planted in your heart
the tree of love,
in hope of nourishment
from that dark cloud.
Now water it
with your tears,

says Govinda-dāsa.

Māna

In pique and anger, Rādhā speaks to Krishna

The marks of fingernails are on your breast
and my heart burns.
Kohl of someone's eyes upon your lips
darkens my face.
I am awake all night;
your eyes are red.
So why do you entreat me, Kān,
saying that you and I have but one heart?
You come with choking voice
while I want to weep.
"Only our bodies are apart."
But mine is light,
and yours is dark.
Go home, then,

says Govinda-dāsa.

May none other be born to this world. But if it must
                          be,
let it not be a girl that is born.
But if a girl must be born, let her not know
the agony that is called 'love.'
But if she must know it, let her not be
a girl of gentle breeding.
Wretched women pray for one thing: God,
let me know peace at last. Let me unite
with a husband wise and skilled, a fountain of love,
and let his love not fall into the power of another.
But if it does, may he be considerate,
for a woman is not wholly lost if she is treated with
                          kindness.

Vidyāpati says: There is a way.
By your own life you can gain the far shore of this
sea of conflict.

Māna

As Rādhā speaks, she realizes the depth
of her love for Krishna

Suddenly I am afraid.
At any moment, Kānu's love for me may cease.
A building can collapse because of a single flaw—
who knows in what ways I, who desire to be
a palace for his pleasure, may be faulty?
And few are those who can restore
what once is broken . . .
Distracted, I wander
from place to place, everywhere finding
only anxiety. Oh, to see
his smile!
      My love,
whoever brings down the house of our love
will have murdered a woman!

Chandidāsa says, O Rādhā, you reflect too much;
without your love he could not live a moment.

My faults, my jealousy, are
woman's nature—
O my heart, Kānāi,
do not be angry.
Did not you, yourself,
use the same words—
'Do not be angry'?—
and now all my anger is gone.
See, awakening at your feet,
my heart, Kānāi. Ah,
do not think of others as you do of me,
the god of love has woven in a garland
your heart and mine,
and I will do as you desire, in Vrindāvana.
Has not God made one body and one soul
of your love and mine? Then it is not my doing
if you must not take your love to another,
but the will of God . . .
One by one I turn your virtues over in my mind—
come, sit beside me,

sings Baru Chandidāsa.

I who body and soul
am at your beck and call,
was a girl of noble family.
I took no thought for what would be said of me,
I abandoned everything:
now I am part of you,
your will is my will.
O Mādhava, never let our love
seem to grow stale—
I beg you, let the dew
not dry on our flowers,
that my honor be not destroyed.

When he heard these words from her beautiful
                          mouth, Mādhava
bowed his head. He knew he held
the flower of her life in his keeping.

Milan

Rādhā, reconciled, returns to Krishna,
and the lovers are united once again

He speaks:

My moon-faced one,
I am waiting
>to make our bed ready,
>to gather lotus petals—
your body will press them,
hidden from even friendly eyes . . .
Come,
the sweet breeze from the sandalwoods
censes our trysting place . . .

Her friend speaks:

Her cloud of hair eclipses the luster of her face,
> like Rāhu greedy for the moon;
the garland glitters in her unbound hair, a wave of
> the Ganges in the waters of the Yamunā.
How beautiful the deliberate, sensuous union of the
> two; the girl playing this time the active role,
riding her lover's outstretched body in delight;
her smiling lips shine with drops of sweat; the god
> of love offering pearls to the moon.
She of beautiful face hotly kisses the mouth of her
> beloved; the moon, with face bent down,
> drinks of the lotus.
The garland hanging on her heavy breasts seems like
> a stream of milk from golden jars.
The tinkling bells which decorate her hips sound the
> triumphal music of the god of love.

She speaks:

Beloved, what more shall I say to you?
In life and in death, in birth after birth
you are the lord of my life.
A noose of love binds
my heart to your feet.
My mind fixed on you alone, I have offered you
                              everything;
in truth, I have become your slave.
In this family, in that house, who is really mine?
Whom can I call my own?
It was bitter cold, and I took refuge
at your lotus feet.
While my eyes blink, and I do not see you,
I feel the heart within me die.

A touchstone
I have threaded, and wear upon my throat,
says Chandidāsa.

She speaks:

Let the earth of my body be mixed with the earth
my beloved walks on.
Let the fire of my body be the brightness
in the mirror that reflects his face.
Let the water of my body join the waters
of the lotus pool he bathes in.
Let the breath of my body be air
lapping his tired limbs.
Let me be sky, and moving through me
that cloud-dark Shyāma, my beloved.

Govinda-dāsa says, O golden one,
Could he of the emerald body let you go?

Mathurā

Krishna has left Vrindāvana for Mathurā, and Rādhā laments

O my friend, my sorrow is unending.
It is the rainy season, my house is empty,
the sky is filled with seething clouds,
the earth sodden with rain,
and my love far away.

Cruel Kāma pierces me with his arrows:
the lightning flashes, the peacocks dance,
frogs and waterbirds, drunk with delight,
call incessantly—and my heart is heavy.
Darkness on earth,
the sky intermittently lit with a sullen glare . . .

Vidyāpati says,
How will you pass this night without your lord?

What avails the raincloud
that only passes over, and leaves the seedlings to scorch?
Or a painted likeness of your lover
if you are far from him all the days of your youth?
The sea on every side, but no water
to quench your thirst.
Such is my fate.
The sandal tree has lost its fragrance,
the touchstone has lost its magic,
the moon rains fire.
Such is my fate.
The clouds of Shrāvan give no rain,
the *sur* tree bears no fruit,
the servant of Him-who-holds-the-mountain
finds no refuge.

Strange this fate seems to Vidyāpati.

Sammilan

Rādhā hears that Krishna will return;
she rejoices at their reunion

When my beloved returns to my house
I shall make my body a temple of gladness,
I shall make my body the altar of joy
and let down my hair to sweep it.
My twisting necklace of pearls shall be the intricate
sprinkled design on the altar,
my full breasts the water jars,
my curved hips the plantain trees,
the tinkling bells at my waist the young shoots of the
    mango.
I shall use the arcane arts of fair women in all lands
to make my beauty outshine a thousand moons.

Soon your hopes, O Rādhā, says Vidyāpati,
will be fulfilled, and he will be at your side.

The moon has shone upon me,
the face of my beloved.
O night of joy!

Joy permeates all things.
My life: joy,
my youth: fulfillment.

Today my house is again
home,
   today my body is
my body.
       The god
of destiny smiled on me.
No more doubt.

Let the nightingales sing, then,
let there be myriad
rising moons, let Kāma's
five arrows become five thousand
and the south wind

softly, softly blow:
for now my body has meaning
in the presence of my beloved.

*Vidyāpati says, Your luck is great;
may this return of love be blessed.*

Nibedan

*A prayer to Krishna, the finite and
the infinite, the mighty God*

Children, wife, friend—
drops of water on heated sand.
I spent myself on them, forgetting you.
What are they to me now,
O Mādhava, now that I am old and without hope,
apart from you. But you are the savior of the world
and full of mercy.
                    Half my life I passed in sleep—
my youth, now my old age,
how much time.
I spent my youth in lust and dissipation.
I had no time to worship you.
                    Ageless gods
have come and passed away.
Born from you, they enter you again
like waves into the sea.
For you have no beginning, and no end.
                                        Now
at the end, I fear
the messengers of Death.
Apart from you, there is no way.
I call you Lord,
the infinite and finite,
my salvation.

NOTES

ON TRANSLATION AND TRANSLITERATION

A problem, inescapable when translating from non-European languages, is that of transliteration. However free one is in translation, there are always names, epithets, and words for concepts and objects for which there are simply no equivalents in English. For the Sanskritic languages there is a conventional transliteration which represents adequately the orthography of the original. For a specialized audience, the use of such a system is perhaps desirable. But for a non-specialized one it is perhaps better to approximate, rather than force the reader to learn a rather elaborate system of diacritics and the sounds, different from those of English, which these diacritics represent. We have therefore, except in citing names of books, and in technical terms, reduced the transliteration system to a single indispensable diacritic: the macron (⁻) over the vowel *a*. When the macron is used, the sound is much like the English "f*a*ther." When the macron is not used, the sound is, in Sanskritic pronunciation, much like the English "but," or, in Bengali pronunciation, that sound represented by the letter sequence "aw" in English "law." A further compromise has been made. In strict transliteration, the vowels "i" and "u" can also appear with a macron. No distinction is made, however, in modern Bengali speech between *i* and *u*, etc.; we have therefore, except in names and technical terms, dispensed with the macron in all cases except *ā*, just as we have represented three orthographically distinct sibilants by *sh*, in an approximation of modern standard speech.

The lyrics vary rather widely in length, as will be clear from the translations, ranging usually between six and sixteen lines. Their meters are regular, and are of two general types, *payār*, a couplet form usually of sixteen metrical units with caesura after the first eight, with the rhyme scheme a–a, b–b, etc., and *tripadi*. The *tripadi* ("three part line"), unlike the rather more pedestrian *payār*, is capable of considerable elegance and variation. The potential rhyme schemes, for example, are many: a–b–c, a–b–c; a–a–b, c–c–b, etc.

Although the meter is extremely regular and subject to the limitations imposed by very stringent rules and poetic conventions, internal devices such as alliteration, which some of the poets used with great skill, and the fact that the lyrics are sung, save them from monotony. The fact that they are sung, with shortness or length of syllables becoming thus a function of music as well as of poetic convention, also presents the translator with the problem of compensation. Because of the variable introduced by the music, it is not possible, even if it were desirable, adequately to represent the original by emulating the regularity of its meter. We have attempted to compensate by a free arrangement of line lengths, though thereby the shape of the poem becomes quite different from that of the original.

A second liberty we have taken is the occasional expansion in the poem itself of terms which for a

Bengali reader need no expansion. A Bengali, for example, would know that a *chakora* bird is supposed to subsist on moonbeams, and it would be redundant for the poet to say so. Most readers of English, however, are less familiar with such conventions, and a line like ". . . chakora birds whose sole food / is moonbeams" is not, in English, redundant. This is less freedom of translation than it is an attempt to give the non-Bengali reader the same experience as the Bengali gets.

Selections are drawn from a variety of printed sources. These sources, with their identifying abbreviations, are:

a. *Padakalpataru* (PKT), edited by Shatishchandra Rāy (Calcutta: Bangiya sāhitya parishad, 5 volumes, 1915–31): an anthology of Vaishnava lyrics, compiled by Vaishnava-dāsa in the middle of the eighteenth century; the fifth volume of this edition contains excellent notes and a Brajabuli-to-modern Bengali glossary.

b. *Vaishnava-padāvali* (VP), edited by Khagendranath Mitra, et al. (Calcutta: Calcutta University, 1952).

c. *Vaishnava-padāvali* (VPM), edited by Harekrishna Mukhopādhyāya (Calcutta: Sāhitya samsad, 1961).

d. *Vaishnava-padāvali* (Sen), edited by Sukumar Sen (New Delhi: Sāhitya Akademi, 1957).

e. *Vidyāpati-gīta-samgraha* (Jha), or *The Songs of Vidyāpati*, edited by Subhadra Jhā (Banaras: Motilal Banarasidass, 1954). Based on an unusual Nepali manuscript, the book has text in Devanagari script and English translation.

f. *Vaishnava-padalahari*, edited by Durgadās Lahiri (Calcutta: N. B. Cakravarti, 1905).

ON VAISHNAVA DOCTRINE

The theology of the Vaishnavas of Bengal is systematic and complex and consists of far more than the charming allegories of the lyric poetry. Sushil Kumar De has given a descriptive and historical account of it in his *Vaishnava Faith and Movement,* and the interested reader is urged toward that excellent book. There is one point, however, which needs clarification here.

As Chaitanya does not enter into the history and doctrine of the *bhakti* movements in other parts of India to anywhere near the same extent as he does in that of Bengal, so the love of Rādhā and the Gopīs for Krishna occupies a peculiarly important place in Bengali Vaishnava thought.

It is difficult to place Rādhā historically. She is not mentioned by name in the *Bhāgavata-purāna,* which in all other ways is crucial to the development of the Vaishnavism of Bengal. She seems to appear first in Bengal in the Sanskrit lyric verse of the poet Dimboka early in the twelfth century, and some years later in the *Gītagovinda* of Jayadeva. In Jayadeva's poems she is the embodiment of the selfless love of all the Gopīs and she remains so in all the poetry and legend of Bengal from that time on.

The tenth book of the *Bhāgavata-purāna,* while not mentioning Rādhā specifically, is full of stories about the variety and intensity of the Gopīs' love for Krishna. Many of these stories are ingenuous and charming, and to the exegeticist extremely troublesome: for the *Bhāgavata-purāna* refers to the Gopīs being the wives of others at the time when they fell in love with Krishna. The theologians, of course, extending themselves, found many interesting explanations for this: that the Gopīs had never consummated their marriages with their husbands, that Krishna had by his magical power caused the Gopīs to be replaced by likenesses of themselves at crucial moments, etc. None of the poets paid much attention to this. To them, it is well that the Gopīs—and by extension Rādhā—were the wives of others. For if a woman is *parakiyā,* a woman in love with one who is not her husband, a greater tension is established, with the necessities of separation and the intensity of emotion that this involves. From a doctrinal point of view also, a *parakiyā* woman giving herself to her lover best illustrates the principle of selfless love, for she has everything to lose.

Not all the Vaishnava lyrics in Bengali treat of the divine love of Rādhā and Krishna. In some songs Krishna the child is celebrated, or Krishna the supreme God, or Krishna the slayer of demons. But for some reason, Krishna the divine lover found Bengal especially congenial, and it is in Bengal that the gentle allegory is preserved with greatest warmth and feeling and detail.

As the *bhanitās* of the poems indicate, the Vaishnava poets very often participate in the actions and emotional attitudes which their poems describe. The condition in which the worshiper, or in this case the poet, knows the immediacy of Krishna, is known as *bhāva*. It is a condition reached by religious training and discipline: participating in *kīrtan,* listening to the reading of the *Bhāgavata,* "serving the feet" of the spiritual guide or *guru,* serving the image of Krishna, meditation on the stories of Krishna, and various other ritual actions. Such actions, if repeated long and often enough, bring about a permanent mental state appropriate to them. In all ritual activity, the worshiper concentrates upon whichever participant in the Krishna story his own personality fits. By playing the role of parent or friend or servant (which three *bhāvas* are less important to Bengali Vaishnavas than to the Hindi poets of northern India), or, as is the case with most of the Bengali poets, the lover, the worshiper in time knows in himself the surpassing depths of emotion experienced by these intimates of the Lord.

The most intimate and passionate of the persons of the Krishna story are of course the lovers of Krishna; thus, the Bengali Vaishnavas consider this *bhāva* the best. Many of the lyric writers speak as Gopīs, in love with Krishna, pleasing him by their love, and looking on, unselfishly pleased, at his lovemaking with Rādhā. Others, in the ultimate *bhāva,* sometimes seem to have become Rādhā herself; her passion for Krishna is theirs.

ON THE POETS

The question of the authorship of Vaishnava poetry is a vexing one, despite the fact of the convention of the *bhanitā* or signature line. First of all, it was—and remains—customary to take a religious name, usually one ending with -*dāsa,* "servant," when becoming a Vaishnava. Thus, the anthologies teem with "Chaitanya-dāsa"s, "Krishna-dāsa"s, and so on: it is often impossible to tell which of many people with the same religious name wrote the poem in question. Secondly, there was in medieval Bengal much less pride of authorship than there is in the modern West. A later poet was very apt to adopt and to sign the name of an earlier and prestigious one to his own work, sometimes with no other end in view than the promulgation of his own particular religious position. These habits annoy modern scholars who do not like to leave loose ends, and are particularly vexing with regard to the two most popular Vaishnava lyric writers, who are properly most extensively represented in this book, "Chandidāsa" and "Vidyāpati."

Textual scholarship has only recently recognized the fact that there were at least two major poets who used the *bhanitā* "Chandidāsa." This recognition has not been due primarily to the fact of the differing *bhanitās* "Dvija Chandidāsa," "Baru Chandidāsa," etc., for the possibility is always there that these two are the same poet, the same too as "Chandidāsa," with the differing signatures due to the poet's stylistic choice or the requirements of meter. It was, however, noticed that the religious viewpoints offered by certain of the poems signed with one or another of the permutations of "Chandidāsa" were those of a theologically deviant group within the general Vaishnava context, called "Vaishnava-sahajiyās." Fine points of doctrine and historical scholarship aside, two "Chandidāsa"s were thus distinguished, the theory being that the later one (late sixteenth or early seventeenth century) signed the name of the earlier (early or middle fifteenth century, at the latest) to his poems because the earlier one had been "read with pleasure" by Chaitanya, and had thus acquired great prestige. The questions of whether or not there were more than two such poets and of dating are still hotly debated subjects among scholars.

The case is similar for the other great pre-Chaitanya non-Sanskrit writer Vidyāpati. A few things are certain. Vidyāpati was a court poet to a king or kings of Mithila, an area just to the west of Bengal as defined on modern maps. He was also, judging from the precision and classical character of many of the poems attached to his name, a scholar of Sanskrit. Other theories about him, such as the one which suggests that he was the recipient of a grant recorded on a copper plate and dated A.D. 1400, are still being argued. And, to complicate the issue, many of the poems which appear in some collections with his name, occur in others with such signatures as "Sekhara."

Fortunately, it is not necessary to know biographical facts about a poet to appreciate his poetry. But although some of the above problems remain, they are considerably lessened in the period following Chaitanya. The reason is that in this period there was an unprecedented spate of historical and biographical writing by the Vaishnavas, with lists of names, activities, and some hints as to the identity of individual men and women prominent in the movement. Although the difficulties caused by religious names persist, in many cases there is a reasonable certainty that people identified by the histories and biographies include the poets represented in this book. Rāmānanda Rāya, for example, who wrote in both Sanskrit and Brajabuli, was a high-ranking political officer of the king Pratāparūdra of Orissa, who ruled from 1504–32; he met and was profoundly influenced by Chaitanya, as we are told in the great biography of the latter, the *Chaitanyacharitāmrita* by Krishna-dāsa. Balārāmadāsa also lived in the early sixteenth century, near Krishnagar in Bengal, and was a Brahman, according to the narrative texts: there are also two other devotees of the same name mentioned, however. A great deal is known about Locana-dāsa, who was himself a biographer of Chaitanya: he was born about 1523, in a village in Burdwan district, and his lineage on both sides of his family, as well as his *guru* (a great Vaishnava apostle named Narahari Sarkār) are known, as are various facts of his life. Biographical sketches of all the poets represented in this book can be found in Sukumar Sen's *History of Brajabuli Literature* (Calcutta: University of Calcutta, 1935).

NOTES TO THE POEMS

On p. 3: "After long sorrow . . ." *PKT*, no. 1994. In the life of Chaitanya (who was also called Gaura, "the golden one"), there were seen many parallels to the love affair of Rādhā or the Gopīs and Krishna. For example, when Chaitanya became a mendicant ascetic, his companions in Navadvip wept in their pain of separation from him, their *viraha,* as the Gopīs wept when Krishna left them to go to Mathurā. And when, before his final departure for Puri, he returned home for a visit with his family and friends, they rejoiced, as the Gopīs rejoiced at the prospect of Krishna's return and their reunion with him. *Chakora* birds are fabled birds said to subsist on moonbeams; the face of Chaitanya, in an ancient image, is "beautiful as the golden moon."

On p. 4: "It was in bitter maytime . . ." *PKT*, no. 1711. "Maytime" is figurative: Māgh, the month specifically mentioned in the poem, is January-February, one of the most delightful times of year in Bengal; the figure yields the type of paradox of which the Vaishnava poets are particularly fond. Chaitanya donned the ascetic's robes when he was about twenty-three years old. The poet,

Rāmānanda, was an early follower of Chaitanya in Navadvip, and very possibly speaks from firsthand experience of the despair which he expresses. Gadādhara, who enters into the signature line, was also one of Chaitanya's early and intimate friends and disciples, who, after Chaitanya's death, gained a very considerable following of his own.

On p. 7: "The girl and the woman . . ." *PKT*, no. 104. Adolescence, according to some Indian erotics, is a particularly attractive phase in a girl's physical development. There is, as usual, a play on the word *kāma* or *Kāma* (there are no capital letters in Bengali). Kāma is the god of love, "the bodiless one," "the one born in the mind," whose body was destroyed by the fiery wrath of Shiva when he tried to tempt that great god from meditation. *Kāma* also means sexual passion or desire.

On p. 8: "Her slender body . . ." *VP*, p. 35. The imagery of the poem is in large part conventional. A body "like a flash of lightning" is one brilliant in color, supple, and graceful. "Feet the color of dawn": in many parts of India, henna is used by women and girls as a cosmetic, to color the feet and the palms of the hands red. Arching brows suggest the shape of the taut bow of Kāma the god of love, ready to let fly the arrow of infatuation; the raising of the brow is an erotic gesture, as is, in some situations, the wink. In the raising of the brow the poet also sees the rising waves of the beautiful dark river Kālindī (another name for the Yamunā, and the name itself suggests the blackness and delicacy of the beautiful brow). Kān and Rāi are intimate and affectionate names for Krishna and Rādhā respectively.

On p. 11: "Fingering the border . . ." *VPM,* p. 585.

On p. 15: "As the mirror to my hand . . ." *VP,* p. 40. The poem bases itself upon the doctrine that Rādhā and Krishna are one soul in two bodies. Krishna incarnated himself in this way because he wanted to experience the depth of Rādhā's love for him. Rādhā is thus a part of Krishna, in some incomprehensible way inseparable from him, "as the scent is inseparable from the flower." *Tāmbul* is a mixture of various nuts, lime, and other aromatic and sweet or pungent substances wrapped in a leaf of the betel tree; when it is chewed, it stains the mouth red, as well as being pleasant to the taste. The word here translated "heart" is literally a peculiar abstraction meaning something like "essence." "Mādhava" is an epithet of Krishna usually used in the context of Krishna as the mighty god rather than the gentle lover. "Kohl" is collyrium, applied around the eyes of women as a cosmetic, and around those of children as both a cosmetic and a medicinal ointment.

On p. 16: "Love, I take on splendor . . ." *VP,* p. 84.

On p. 17: "As water to sea creatures . . ." *VPM,* p. 205. *Chakora* birds are said to subsist on moonbeams. The moon, according to Indian fancy, is full of nectar, and the mark or stain upon it, "the man in the moon" as it is often called in the West, is a deer or a rabbit. The moon's stain also gives rise to a traditional figure of the beauty of the face of the beloved: "the moon seems stained, when seen beside her face." The lines "My body . . . twin of flesh" rest upon two points of doctrine. The first is that the body and its image (Krishna and Rādhā) are somehow one. The second, related to this, is that the self is a reflection of the Self, in the Emersonian sense: without the presence of Krishna, who is reality, there can be no mirror image or reflection. The lines "His life . . . the moon" call to mind another favorite image of the Vaishnava poets: the stain of her "adultery," as the world calls it, upon Rādhā.

On p. 18: "My friend, I cannot answer . . ." *VPL*, p. 94. The love of Rādhā and Krishna is eternal, and the two are in essence one. The term "subtle people" is a translation of *rasika*—those who really know how to nourish and appreciate the subtle emotions and refinements of life in general and of love in particular. "To cool" is in all Indian languages pretty much what it is in English: "to soothe, quiet, calm down," to escape the heat of passion, or, more earthily, the heat of the sun or the very common fevers. Coolness is a sensation which only people living in tropical countries can really appreciate.

On p. 21: "O Mādhava, how shall I tell you . . ." *VP*, p. 58.

On p. 22: "This dark cloudy night . . ." *VP*, p. 74.

On p. 23: "When they had made love . . ." *VPM*, p. 52. The poem is based upon a fundamental

Vaishnava notion that death is latent in life, that pain is latent in pleasure, and that, as here, separation is latent in union. The poem also shows the Vaishnava fondness for paradox, observing that extremity of pain keeps one from fainting with pain. Here too is a rather typical expression of the futile but very human search afar for what is near at hand: God is within, and one need only look there to find him. *Kunja* is a grove, bowered with flowering creepers and plants. The *anchal* is the corner of the sari which is worn over the shoulder, into which women in Bengal tie money and other valuables. The signature line is interesting. The poet Govindadāsa is speaking as one of the companions of Rādhā, one of the Gopīs, who are often present at these intimate scenes. Here the passion of the scene is evidently such that even the Gopīs are embarrassed and go away; a frequent fancy in erotic poetry is that even Kāma the love god takes his wife Rati by the hand and withdraws from a scene of intense passion.

On p. 24: "Lord of my heart, what have I dreamed . . ." *VPM*, p. 190. The scene takes place in the flower grove (*kunja*); Rādhā is awakening from sleep after an amorous night. In Bengal, a line of vermilion in the part of the hair is a mark of a married woman. "Down-glancing one" is a traditional epithet of Krishna; in the conventional figure, the arched brow is compared to the taut bow of the god of love, ready to shoot the arrow of the flirtatious or infatuating glance. Krishna's robes, like Rādhā's body, are yellow, and he always wears a garland of forest flowers. "Someone in Gokula" is Rādhā; Gokula is one of the names (others being

"Vrindāvana" and, more generally, "Vraja") of the area near Mathurā in which the idyll takes place.

On p. 27: "With the last of my garments . . ." *Jha*, no. 57. "The Mind-stealing One" is Kāma, the god of love. *Chātaka* birds are said to subsist on raindrops. In the Brajabuli of the original, the sex of the person who is "leaning across" or "gazing at" the lamp is not entirely clear. We have chosen to interpret the poem as the reaction of a reluctant or unwilling Rādhā to Krishna's advances. This interpretation seems to fit with the final lines. The *bhanita* reads: "So Vidyāpati says."

On p. 28: "O, why did I go to the Yamunā river . . ." *VPM*, p. 877. Nanda is the name of the foster-father of Krishna. The *kadamba* tree is a flowering tree with brilliant, fragrant, yellow-colored blossoms, with which the banks of the Yamunā are bowered. It was usual in India, when hunting birds, to set bait on the ground beneath a tree and then, when the birds alighted, to cast a net over them. *Dharma* is best understood here as "that which is proper"; people should subordinate themselves to the role in society decreed by their birth and station. Thus Rādhā should be modest, self-effacing, and subservient to the wish or word of her father or husband. The *tribhanga* ("bent in three") pose is that in which Krishna is most often seen, with his body bent at the neck, waist, and with one leg, bent at the knee, crossed over the other. The posture is reminiscent of a drawn bow. The *bhanita* reads "So says Jagadānanda-dāsa."

On p. 29: "How can I describe . . ." *VPM*, p. 57. The image of women being dragged by the hair is even more extreme than it appears in English. Since according to custom the hair should not be touched, the suggestion is that the women are seized any old way, against their will, in great agitation, and that they cannot resist; the suggestion is also that Krishna has little concern for the social niceties. The "clinging vines" have a personalizing suffix in the Bengali, and are the Gopīs. Kālā is "the dark one," Krishna.

On p. 30: "My mind is not on housework . . ." *VP,* p. 78.

On p. 31: "I brought honey . . ." *VPM,* p. 65. "Sin," *pāpa,* has nothing to do with that condition as it is defined by Christian doctrine. In general, the meaning of *pāpa* is something closer to "wickedness," although there is an undertone: in the Vaishnava context, *pāpa* is the absence of Krishna from the worshiper's life, or the worshiper's denial of Krishna (here called by the affectionate name Kānu).

On p. 32: "Love, what can I say to you? . . ." *VP,* p. 75. The *kadamba* tree is flowered with brilliant yellow blossoms, and forests the banks of the Yamunā river. *Tribhanga* ("bent in three") is the favorite pose of Krishna as he plays his flute: his body is bent at the neck, waist, and knee; see the note on poem on p. 28.

On p. 33: "A wicked woman . . ." *VPM,* p. 748.

On p. 37: "I place beauty spots . . ." The poem is by Vidyāpati, and is from an anthology of his poems having the nearly standard *bhanita* line "So

Vidyāpati says." This anthology is also one which, in the printed book at least, is without section identification; putting this poem under *Āptadūtī* is therefore to a certain extent speculation. *Alake* seems to mean locks of hair turned down to frame and beautify the face; another possibility, however, is that it means "beauty spots," a cosmetic device used especially as decoration for a bride (this meaning yields an additional note of irony). *Pakalā kesha,* literally "cooked hair," is a perfectly ordinary idiomatic phrase signifying "gray hair." A term closer to the literal seemed better to us in the context, as underscoring the image of a body burned out by the fire of passion. In the final line, the word translated as "the God of Love" is *ananga,* "the bodiless one."

On p. 38: "Shining one, golden as the *champa* flower . . ." *VPM,* p. 466.

On p. 41: "From the time our eyes first met . . ." *VPM,* p. 136. "He of the five arrows" is Kāma, the god of love. Kāma holds a bow and five arrows made of flowers, namely delight, infatuation, absorption in love, immersion in love, and complete joy. The poem also employs the conceit of the "Gandharva" form of marriage, a love marriage which requires the presence of none but the bride and groom at the ceremony. It is often said that at a Gandharva marriage, Kāma is the priest, the six seasons are the wedding guests, and Rati, Kāma's wife, is the attendant of the bride. The signature line of the poem is a complete pun, and can be read either, as here, "So, with anger like a king's, increasing . . .", or, "So, in homage to the king Pratāparūdra, who grows in might . . ." The Mahārājā Pratāparūdra was the patron of the poet.

On p. 42: "When you listened to the sound . . ." *VPM*, p. 625.

On p. 45: "The marks of fingernails . . ." *PKT*, no. 423.

On p. 46: "May none other be born . . ." *Jha*, no. 53. The term here translated "God" is *vidhātā*, a name of God as the creator and the disposer of the fates of men.

On p. 49: "Suddenly I am afraid . . ." *VPM*, p. 59. The murder of Brahmans, cows, or women (in that order), is one of the most heinous crimes imaginable.

On p. 50: "My faults, my jealousy . . ." *VPM*, p. 36. Kānāi is an affectionate name for Krishna. Vrindāvana is the forested place in which Rādhā and Krishna meet. "God" is *vidhātā;* see the note to poem on page 46.

On p. 51: "I who body and soul . . ." *Jha*, no. 231. The *bhanita* reads "Love with a good man, says Vidyāpati, lasts to the end."

On p. 55: "My moon-faced one . . ." *VPM*, p. 135. The *bhanita* reads, "So sings the poet Rāmānanda Rāya, that pleasure be brought to the heart of the great king Pratāparūdra." The poem is in Sanskrit, and is in fact imbedded in a Sanskrit drama by Rāmānanda. One commentator notes that sometimes, when the poem is included in anthologies, it occurs in the *pūrva-rāga* section, and sometimes it appears in *māna*. We have taken the liberty of placing it between *māna* and *milan*.

On p. 56: "Her cloud of hair . . ." *Jha,* no. 159. It is said that an eclipse is caused by a demon called Rāhu, who eats the moon. The waters of the Ganges are light in color, while those of the Yamunā are dark. "Tinkling bells" is a suggestive phrase. Women wore ornamental girdles around their hips, which tinkled pleasantly with their movements. The *bhanita* reads, "So Vidyāpati says."

On p. 57: "Beloved, what more shall I say . . ." *VP,* no. 72. The conceit of the blinking of an eye seeming an eternity is an old and conventional one.

On p. 58: "Let the earth of my body . . ." *VP,* p. 96. All material nature is made up of the five elements: earth, fire, water, air, and sky or space. Rādhā's golden body is the perfect setting for the dark emerald-colored Krishna.

On p. 61: "O my friend, my sorrow is unending. . . ." *VP,* p. 91.

On p. 62: "What avails the raincloud . . ." *VP,* p. 93. The rainy season is the most important time of the year, in Bengal and in all of India, for it brings relief from the vicious sun and makes the earth again fruitful. It is also a time for lovers to be together, a joyful time. The feelings of the people, when the dark monsoon clouds appear in the south, and then pass over without fulfilling their promise, can be imagined. "Shrāvan" is the month July-August, when the monsoon is at its height in Bengal. The *sur* tree, *surtaru*, is the tree of the gods, which bears nectarous fruit. "He who holds the mountain" is Krishna, who protected his people from a storm sent by the angry Indra by holding a mountain over their heads. The moon is as cool as camphor, and as refreshing; the "moon rains fire" is the kind of personal and paradoxical reaction to nature the Vaishnava poets love.

On p. 65: "When my beloved returns . . ." *VP*, p. 101. On festive or ritual occasions, designs are made in auspicious places around the house. These designs, stylized and intricate, are drawn with white rice powder by the women of the house. Water jars, plantain stalks, and mango shoots are also parts of the ritual paraphernalia. A woman's breasts compared to water jars is a usual enough figure, suggested by similarity of shape, although the water pot as a symbol of fertility is very ancient. Plantain trees, curved and full, are often compared to a woman's hips and thighs. For comment on "tinkling bells," see the notes to poem on p. 56; throughout, there is a suggestion of the Gandharva form of marriage—see the note to poem on p. 41.

On p. 66: "The moon has shown upon me . . ." *VP*, p. 102.

On p. 69: "Children, wife, friend . . ." *VPM*, p. 131. The poem is by Vidyāpati.